DYNAMICS OF PRAYER

By Mary Saurer-Smith

CONTENTS

INTRODUCTION

Looking at ancient cultures around the world we can see that the urge to pray is an instinct of the human mind. That is because the Holy Spirit within is urging us to seek communion with our Source. Prayer is communion with God, the Source of all that is. The result of frequent prayer is a habit of praying.

One who has a habit of praying daily has developed an ongoing prayer consciousness which is the awareness of prayer as a partnership with God.

Increasing one's prayer consciousness expands faith, inner peace, and a deeper sense of spiritual happiness. Since I started teaching these concepts, over 40 years ago, I have used my personal experiences of prayer and meditation as the foundation for classes and for my continued spiritual development. God does not change. God is as God is;

regardless of what name is given, regardless of what sacrifices and rituals are practiced or not practiced, and regardless of what concept one might hold of the definition and nature of God. God is the constant in our lives. Our concepts of God, our concept of prayer and our practices change as we evolve. Even the name we use for God might change, but God remains the same.

One of my objectives for this book is to expose the reader to an explanation of prayer that will increase your understanding, increase your faith, and empower you to experience more effectiveness in your own prayer life. This book can be easily adapted to classroom teaching, or to self-education if a teacher is not desired or not available.

The difference between persons who fear God and those who love God without fear is a personal consciousness of the eternal Presence of the Holy Spirit within themselves. It includes a growth in understanding that the nature of God, the powers of God and all the qualities of God are creative and constructive.

Prayer produces a growing sense of intimacy with God as a partner in support of the Divine Plan and the Source of the Holy Spirit within each person. The result is an increasing expansion of inner peace. That change in you is the magic of prayer as it becomes an imperishable sense of beauty in you.

When you pray, you want your prayers to be effective and not just a lot of words. Your faith in prayer increases through belief that someone or something is receiving your communication. All it takes to assure that every prayer is effective is to acknowledge your awareness of the Divine Presence. That awareness is established when you address the Divine Presence by whatever name you use for God. The initial effect of prayer is to place the praying person and the object of the prayer

in the stream of Divine Order, but there are degrees of effectiveness.

LESSON ONE
WHAT IS PRAYER

Seven Practices that condition your consciousness for the most effective prayer:

Practice # 1. Acknowledge God as your Divine Source of formless Good. Be Grateful

This does not mean that God suddenly favors you and gives you special rewards because you show gratitude. It means that God is Divine Mind and there is a Power in Divine Mind that honors harmless, creative, constructive thought and action.

In Divine Mind, constructive, creative action is always in harmony with our Creator's Divine Plan and Ultimate Purpose. The plan is that, through our earthly experience and our communion with God, every individual will have ample opportunity to evolve in Spiritual Awareness, Spiritual Understanding and Spiritual Character.

Your mind is an energy field, and it is made of the same energy as Divine Mind. Your freedom to use that energy is what gives you and others the liberty to support the Divine Plan as they perceive it, or to insist on a different Way.

The Divine Intelligence in you provides you with the awesome ability to think, to compare, and to consciously create images and ideas with your mind. You soon become conscious that knowledge gained in prayer has the power to help shape your experiences. You become aware that you have the ability to seek and find answers to your instinctive questions about the meaning and purpose for life, and to consciously make choices in your search for fulfillment. This empowers you to be both an observer and a participant in your own life-story, a co-creator with God.

Your whole mind is your eternal soul, and it cannot be separated from God. Not the brain but the

Being that inhabits the brain. The part of your soul that is already perfect is that which the Master, Jesus, referred to as "the upper room." The part of your soul that you take into the upper room for prayer is the conscious power of mind as it contains your will and your power to focus on God. You consciously address the Creator when you move your attention to the "upper room."

The part of your soul that hungers for knowledge, understanding, intimacy and perfection is the subconscious aspect of mind. It holds your memories, the record of your life-story, and it hungers for sustained fulfillment.

As the paradigm in the subconscious changes, so does the level of desperation and frustration. Through the channel of the Holy Spirit, your soul is perpetually connected to the conscious power of Divine Mind. When you are in a prayer consciousness, you are fully conscious of being in intimate communication with God and you feel a sense of peace throughout your soul.

Where and what God is to you would depend on your belief system. Your concept of God does make a difference in your understanding level but does not make a difference in your ability to experience a prayer consciousness.

God is everywhere at all times. In this small book, we will thoroughly explore the question of how one's consciousness of God as a partner can be developed and sustained to produce that ongoing stream of peace in you. The energy of the Holy Spirit within you is the perpetual lifeline between your individual soul and its Source.

Practice #1 summarized: Express Gratitude. Acknowledge that God is the Source of your sustained happiness.

Practice # 2. Acknowledge the constant Presence and Availability of God (you cannot be separated from God).

This means that the Holy Spirit, that stream of Divine energy that flows into your soul, connects you directly to the consciousness of the Source. The upper region of your mind contains the highest vibration of the Divine power that is within you. Because the flowing of the Holy Spirit into you is your direct link to the Being and Consciousness of the Source, it is also your direct link, like a telephone connection, to God.

You can withdraw your conscious attention from God or give your conscious attention to God, but you will never find that God withdraws Divine substance from you. The channel is always open and available to pour more Spiritual Life into you through the open door that you provide when you pray.

Divine Mind is always ready to receive you but does not pursue you. In prayer, you commune with God by the simple act of giving your attention to inspirational thoughts of God and doing the activity of consciously focusing your thoughts on God. It is like inviting God in for a focused visit. This activity temporarily alters the vibration of your conscious aspect of mind, and you find your awareness drifting upward to merge with the pure Divine Intelligence of the Holy Spirit within.

Practice #2 summarized: Acknowledge the constant presence of God.

The result of these first two practices is stimulation of faith in you. That spiritual vibration radiates downward to the subconscious to alter your soul's vibrations during the prayer time. A feeling of peace spreads through your mind and body, and you sense the Presence of God in you and beyond you. The more often you use your will to move into a prayer consciousness, the easier it becomes, and the more frequently you are conscious of being in the current of Divine Order instead of the disturbing social order of this world.

Practice # 3. "Seek first the Kingdom of God."

Do this by closing the door of your attention to all outer sensations and distractions. In that way you can be intimately alone with God, your confidante and counselor. In order to let the inner peace fully be felt in you, and before you begin to speak your prayer, you seek first to experience the nurturing quality and beauty of the Divine Presence. This is not done simply by decision, but by feeling the peace of just being with God. It is like the feeling you might have with a friend who smiles, gives you a hug and says, “Come in.”

Using the same analogy, when you have a need to “talk” to God, your experience of receptivity might be delayed until you “get it off your chest.”

To relieve you of any sense of “forbidden” ways to pray, let me explain. You have heard or read ideas from “positive thinking” religions or individuals that we must not think or speak or feel the “negative” or sorrow filled status of our experiences 6 while in prayer. You have heard or read that we must not tell God of our tragedy, or pain, or fear while in prayer, because God already knows.

It is true that God already knows, but if you think of God as your counselor or closest friend whom you have just invited for some quality time, you would have no reservations about telling a such a friend of your situation as you begin your session. Let me assure you that God has no barriers against what you can and cannot present in communication when you engage in prayer. We go to God in prayer about many things, and sometimes just to experience the peace of prayer consciousness for starting our day. But very often we go to God when we are in grief, or angry. Or we might be feeling a sense of loss or confusion, or a need of some kind. Just as it is with an effective grief counselor or empathetic friend, we find we can objectify the burden by describing how we feel and talking about what has stimulated this disturbance in our minds. In the telling, a feeling of intimacy is established. Your sense of intimacy with God increases the prayer consciousness.

Telling about your situation changes it from the feeling stage, into words that identify it more objectively. God is a good listener, and even an active listener if you are paying attention to the Divine responses. There is nothing you are forbidden to say to God. Your sense of guilt or fear going in, will never interfere with the results of your prayer unless you keep holding onto them after you have told them to God. Even if you take them back after prayer, it is important to have given them to God at some point during the prayer. Sometimes a confession or the telling of the story is needed to settle the emotions down. This helps the vibrations of your subconscious move into a stage of peaceful receptivity.

How you communicate with God is a personal and private issue between you and God. After the "telling," the longer you stay focused on just staying in the inner peace at, or near, the crown of your head, the more you will lose awareness of the outer. With continuation you will temporarily lose awareness of your concerns and human situations. In that moment you will know that God is always available to help you; to commune with you, to nurture and console you, to strengthen and advise you and your sense of appreciation increases.

Practice #3 summarized: Seek a sense of intimacy with God

Practice 3 prepares the consciousness for receptivity by relieving stress and producing peace. It is from a point of peace that we can be sensitive and receptive to guidance, nurturing, and an influx of Divine Intelligence, not only in ourselves but in our outer fields of energy. This exercise produces an altered state of consciousness in which you are keenly aware of God as a Reality for you.

Practice # 4: State your Prayer or Desire in any way that you choose.

Believe that your thoughts, feelings, and desires are being known consciously by God as you think them. This means that once you begin the prayer, your active thoughts and feelings are telepathically transmitted to the Source Mind.

There is a difference between the "telling" of your situation and the prayer itself. Your actual prayer is about the end result as you desire it to be.

The Holy Spirit is your energy link to Divine Mind; so, once you have finished your preliminary communication of the current situation to God, you can state your desire. This stimulates a vibration at the crown of your head. Like a chain reaction, this vibration goes through the Holy Spirit instantly, transmitting your entire message to the consciousness of Divine Mind where it is processed. It is then returned to both you and any other energy fields in the universe that are related to your prayer. You do not have to accept or understand this for it to happen. Just trust in the Light of the Holy Spirit to function as a conductor in transmitting your communications to God; and talk to God with an attitude of trusting that you are heard.

Practice #4 summarized: Believe that God is receiving your prayer.

Practice # 5: Ask for ideas about how to contribute to your desired outcome.

This is the receptive/listening stage of your prayer. It means that after your statements and desires are offered, acknowledge in thought or word that you are now receptive to God's guidance in the matter. Then wait in the silence for a moment (as if listening for a response). Ideas, visions, impressions, or urges might come. If they are from Spirit, they will be experienced in the upper regions of your mind between the center of your forehead and the crown of your head. If they are from your subconscious, they will be sensed in the torso near the heart or solar-plexus area of your body, or the center brain.

Be receptive to ideas from the Holy Spirit with an unspoken commitment to follow through with the Divine ideas that you might receive in regard to your prayer.

Practice #5 summarized: Confirm willingness to be guided and to do your part.

Practices 4 and 5, which are the actual prayer action of talking and listening to God, produce Divine Order for you and the subject of your prayer. God does not dictate how you must present your situation or how you must speak as you pray. Eloquence is not required. Honesty is vital.

Suppressing your feelings is not required. Supplication is not forbidden. Simply make known your desires. If you do the listening step after presenting your request, you might receive insights, impressions, ideas, or visions of how you can contribute to your desired outcome. Divine Order is the stream of life that offers you, and the subject of your prayer, the best opportunities for spiritual growth.

Practice # 6: Offer gratitude for the awesome privilege of communicating directly with God.

You can liken this final step to the way that you would say thank you to a counselor who has given you time, a listening ear, nurturing support, and a few options or ideas to consider. You would not think of leaving the counselor's presence without an expression of gratitude. It is not required by the counselor, but it is an emotional closure for you; a bonding experience for the two of you and an acknowledgment of the help you received. This step makes you feel closer to God even when the prayer is over. It increases your sense of completion.

Practice#6 summarized: Give thanks for the ongoing opportunity to pray.

The result of practice # 6 is to deepen your inner peace and bring closure to the prayer for you. It strengthens your commitment to acceptance of the outcome of your prayer.

Practice # 7: Follow Through with action if that is in order.

Another necessary condition of mind for the most effective prayer and prayer consciousness is to trust that you have received the right response from God. This includes not only the communication part of your prayer, but your follow-through as well, which is in the field of action. A counselor would call it an "assignment;" your part to do.

After the prayer, be sure to follow through with any insights or ideas that came to you as action ideas. The first step in the Divine Order produced by prayer is the "feedback" you receive from God. If no ideas come, there is nothing you are to do about it at this time. But if constructive ideas do come, acting on them is a creative action that contributes to your desired prayer results. Ideas that come through the Holy Spirit are never harmful to anyone nor to they take advantage of another through deceit.

Your response to the ideas received in prayer has power to alter the course of Divine Order for you. In other words, your own involvement or lack of it might circumvent or produce certain "lessons" or opportunities in relation to your prayer. After following through, release it to the field of manifestation. Trust in the outcome, knowing that the actual result will be a point in Divine Order for you or for the targeted recipients of your prayer. Divine Order is not a stable point of experience. It is a point of progress, like a steppingstone in the right direction that takes one to new choices, opportunities and options that might not have encountered without prayer.

Practice #7 summarized: Do your part to contribute to the outcome by the application of ideas that come to you in prayer.

LESSON 2
How does Prayer Work?
(Concepts to contemplate or discuss)

The first impact of prayer is in you. The first effect of Prayer is to alter the vibrations of the praying person's conscious mind. It increases your creative mind power (ability) through the stimulation of your Divine Intelligence and increases your sense of faith through the experience of the Divine Presence within. You literally magnetize and absorb more of the Divine Powers into your conscious mind as you hold your undivided attention upon the Holy Spirit Within. But you are free to use that creative mind power any way that you choose once you "come down" from your immersion in the Presence at the crown. God does not dictate. God suggests, through ideas, urges, impressions, and visions, how to use the power of Divine Intelligence in this situation. God's will is always for constructive, creative application of your God-given powers, but an inseparable part of Divine Intelligence is your power of free will. You are free to give your will over to someone else or to God, but God never requires you to sacrifice your will. It is a choice. The very acts of going to God in prayer and following through after the prayer are acts of will. You can use your personal will to align your actions and choices with God's creative guidance and the Divine Plan as you understand it, or you can use your personal will to try to force outcomes, regardless of how it impacts others in your field of activity. It is a choice. By the action of Universal Law, Divine Order is established for you through the mind action of your prayer, but that Order can be altered in an even more positive way if you function as a co-creator in the situation. You do that by following the ideas that came in prayer, then turn the outcome over to God for fulfillment of Divine Order. Divine Order produces that which is best for your Spiritual progress or Spiritual progress for the subject of your prayer.

If we try to force our desired outcome in rebellion, that mind action or physical action interferes with the natural result of our prayer. We cannot "create" anything at all. We can only contribute to the desired results.

The manifestation is either Divine Order or universal order; Divine Order if prayer is involved, universal or social order if it is not. Doing our part alters the energy combinations in the field of action or field of manifestation. When the vibration of the processed prayer returns from Divine Mind back into the universal field of action, its first manifestation is as a hologram impregnated with pure 10 Divine Vibrations. This produces Divine Order in relation to the prayer.

When we do more than our part by trying to force a desired result. it requires resistance against other energies at work in the field of action (trespassing, competing, or controlling). With forceful effort, we are uniting our will power with the universal order of physical force and opposing forces instead of with God's Order of development. How do we know how much is enough for doing our part and when to let go for the manifestation to occur? You can be certain of what to do and what not to do about the situations that concern you if you pray daily asking for guidance with each prayer. If no guidance comes (no positive, creative, harmless but constructive ideas of what you can do) then do nothing. Divine Order is at work. Give it time. The closer the situation gets to a manifestation point, the less guidance you will receive.

During this development time, new facts or realizations might become evident. Act on them in support of your prayer. If you perceive your part as forcing, manipulating, or interfering with the decisions of another, you are acting on your personal will for the outcome, and not "letting" the other energies play their part in the development. This is not Spiritual guidance, no matter how strongly you might "feel" it. God does not interfere with the free will of anyone with punishment or threat, nor does God guide you to do that. God will guide you to make your own peaceful choices in the situation in response to what another chooses.

Remember that if Divine Order produces a situation that seems like a loss to you and is not at all the outcome for which you prayed, it is actually a point of perfect order in your life's journey; something for you to deal with as a Spiritual being. Keep in mind that you and God are creative partners in your life story and that the goal is progress for you through various stages of evolution in Spiritual consciousness.

If things seem difficult to accept, through Divine Intelligence you can go to God in prayer again and confess that you are confused or disappointed in the current outcome. God never fails to provide nurturing peace when you pray. Once you sense a deeper peace, ask for guidance in taking your next step from that point. When in doubt as to whether it is guidance from God, ask yourself, "Is this a constructive act that will harm no one and will help contribute to my desired result?" If the answer is no, then just hold your peace and be not disturbed. The manifestation of a new point in Divine Order for you is near.

Affirmations and Denials are the Creative Power of Divine Intelligence applied by saying Yes and No. •

Affirmations are the mental application of your mind's will power in relation to ideas that you value. The will power is the power of choice or acceptance. It is your Power to say yes to an idea. •

Denial is another mental application of your mind's will power. It is the ability to say no, to reject, and to cast out an idea.

• Affirmations and Denials result in accepting or rejecting/releasing specific beliefs in the subconscious. Your beliefs are implanted in your mind as self-elected dictatorial rules that govern your thoughts, feelings, behaviors, and future choices. The more harmonious your affirmations and denials are with your ideals, your purpose, your goals in life, and your sense of "self," the more harmonious your subconscious will be with your Holy Spirit. (Obviously, this is simply the exercise of your ability to unite with one idea and release affiliation with another. Using denials for cleansing, and affirmations for re-choosing is how we develop changes in our belief system as well as in our habits and behaviors.)

We can use Affirmations to build Faith and Trust in God. This can be done through words combined with visualization. Exercise: Mentally image your entire mind immersed in the awesome power of the Holy Spirit at the crown of your head, while the energy of Divine Intelligence is flowing into that region of your crown directly from God.

Your consciousness is like a thirsty sponge absorbing the Divine Essence and surrounded by it. With this image then affirm: God is my Creator and my Provider. I cannot be separated from God. Holding your attention upon the effect of that conditioning of the mind, you will soon feel the reality of Divine Peace spread from conscious mind into the subconscious as the feeling descends down through your nervous system to be sensed at the heart region of your body. In this way, peace will flow into your entire mind and body. You will become more conscious of your Faith and with it you will have a deeper desire to bring Divine Power into every situation.

Without faith confirmed through the first 2 steps listed in Lesson 1, a prayer will be greatly less effective for producing exactly what you desire, because faith is the receptive quality of the mind. We amplify the magnetic quality of the Holy Spirit within by consciously acknowledging our reverence and love for God, and our acceptance of the outcome of prayer.

a) We stimulate the Holy Spirit by imaging ourselves being connected to the fullness of God through the Holy Spirit and letting our attention drift gently upward to a place near the crown of the head.
b) The Holy Spirit is our link to God, but we are fully aware of it only when our conscious power of mind is centered in the "Secret Place." When not centered there, our conscious mind might still be aware of the Source, but it will be divided between consciousness of the outer—or of our feelings and thoughts—and consciousness of God.

During prayer, the less keen our awareness of the outer or of the inner mind action, the more we can absorb the full radiance of the Source. The purpose for absorbing this radiance is to empower us to right action, right thinking and right feeling, of course. It is here, in the Upper Room of your mind, that you will start your dialogue with God after you have experienced that shift in awareness that makes you more aware of God and less aware of your inner disturbance.

The shortest distance from consciousness of the human condition to consciousness of the Divine is to use the name of God in a positive affirmation for inspiration

An Exercise:

a) Consider the following affirmations one at a time and let your mind form a picture of them or a feeling about them.
   - I cannot be separated from God.

   - God is the Source of all the Life, Wisdom, Love and Creative Power that I have in me.

   - God is the Source of my will power and my very existence.

   - God is Always Available to Teach me more, to Love Me more and to Guide me through my Journey in the World.

b) Create an affirmation or several affirmations for yourself that contain those ideas.

c) Focus your attention at your throat or your heart and mentally "teach this to your subconscious" by stating your affirmation (s) with confidence. Take time to visualize or feel each statement before you go on to the next.

During this exercise, your conscious mind will become still and mesmerized and focused on witnessing the harmonic interplay of responsive vibrations between the Holy Spirit and the subconscious. This is the Holy Spirit resonating in harmony with your affirmation. Through this "inner dance" that you are witnessing between the subconscious and the Holy Spirit, the vibrations gradually magnetize your conscious attention upward by the vibrating beauty or "music" produced by its wavelike motion.

After a few repetitions of the affirmation, you will sense two things:

a) deepening of inner peace

b) mental and emotional engagement in your experience of

the waves of vibrations between the Holy Spirit and the subconscious (mild euphoria)

Soon you will feel comfort, peace and nurturing energy spreading throughout your entire being, including your body. Every cell and organ, limb and gland will be impacted in a creative way. Focusing on these affirmations of acknowledgment, while holding the attention at the crown, produces a deepening of your conscious awareness of the Divine Intelligence at the crown of your head, and it increases your personal sensation of Spiritual Beauty.

LESSON 3
How do Affirmations or Denials contribute to Purification and Transformation?

New Thought Philosophies and Religions originally taught the power of the mind in using denials and affirmations as a method for purifying the subconscious and keeping it up to date (ridding the subconscious program of old beliefs and implanting new beliefs in their place.) New Thought philosophies were a self-help program for changing the way you think in order to and escalate the spiritual development of your soul. They presented the goal as transformation of the subconscious to the point that it would integrate or be in constant harmony with the Holy Spirit within the superconscious aspect of the mind, near the crown of the head. The Holy Spirit was said to infuse the mind with certain qualities and powers, and Divine Ideals were considered the guidelines or blueprint for our efforts. The concept of the Divine Ideals differed from one New Thought group to another, but the methods of self-help for transformation of the subconscious were the same in New Thought religions. Unfortunately, this is no longer being taught by New Thought religions except by the few surviving ministers who were trained under those concepts. Currently their focus is on social involvement, human bonding, and love rather than seeking personal transformation as before. Denials are a method for purification of error beliefs from the subconscious through the mind's power of releasing or renunciation. The action of denial is orchestrated by the conscious will to withdraw mind energy that has been invested in one idea or belief or concept, so that same mind energy can be reinvested in a different idea or belief. By the creative law at work in the mind, repetitious denials act in the garden of the mind as shovel might act in a physical garden, They "dig" an old belief or attitude or habit out of the subconscious so that the mind energy that was holding that belief as a thought-form in the subconscious is set free and restored ready to be reinvested in a preferred belief. To practice a denial in this context does not mean to "pretend that something does not exist." Nor does it mean to condemn the old idea. It simply means that the conscious mind (observer and decision-power of mind that holds the power of conscious will) chooses to eliminate the selected thought-form from its subconscious program in or a der to replace it with a different thought-form. To prevent resistance that might be caused by this "surgical" activity in the subconscious, you do it in a nurturing and respectful way and not in a forceful or condemning way. You "explain" this choice to your subconscious or inner child The same way you would explain to another person, in a non-threatening, gentle manner: While focusing on the heart or solar plexus area of the body, state firmly but gently that this "was a former belief" but now you are replacing it with a "better" or "new" belief, and that you are acting now on the new belief and will stop giving action power to the old. If the roots are deep (a long-term belief or habit} you will feel resistance and might need to apply the "mental shovel" with its uprooting power every day for a week in order to clear the space for the new implant that you will put in its place. After six weeks of consistent ignoring the old urge and acting on the new, the old belief will take its last breath of life and dissolve. Affirmations are a proven method for implanting accepted beliefs in the subconscious through use of the acceptance and rejection Powers of the conscious will. By the law at work in the mind, a new belief affirmed is like a seed planted in the "garden" of your subconscious. Every repetition of the affirmation is like adding life or "sunlight and water" to that seedling. Acting, speaking, and thinking as if you believe that seed idea acts like nutrients in the ground to the seed idea, or like a magnet uniting the affirmed belief with your action. To practice an affirmation, mentally repeat an idea that you choose to believe. To implant it firmly as a belief in the subconscious, think it over and over and visualize it if you can. Caution: If an affirmation is implanted without first eliminating conflicting or opposing beliefs through the practice of denial, it will not replace the old belief but will co-exist with it as a conflicting belief about the same thing. Beliefs prompt the way we think, feel and act. Inner mental and emotional conflict and much inner argument will ensue when several inner beliefs about the same thing are triggered by outer stimulus all at the same time. To "purify" the consciousness is to eliminate beliefs that conflict with your latest understanding about that question. Purification Exercise The effective prayer technique for freeing yourself of outdated beliefs and self-destructive emotions includes both denials and affirmations. A good technique for this inner purging, or purification of the subconscious, is a full chakra meditation with various Spiritual Qualities or Ideals linked to each chakra or major gland in the body. This concentration on each of the glands amplifies the inner positive energy in the body and brain while using the thought forms of your mind action to "uproot" old beliefs and "plant the seeds" for new beliefs in your subconscious. Your subconscious is your personal operating program in life. Repetitions of this activity for a few weeks' "water" the "seed ideas" to assure that they become strongly rooted in the subconscious and grow into new thought/feeling habits, new attitudes, and new responses to life. God gives us the innovative ideas or confirms ideas for us in the Silence but does not take our old ideas from the subconscious. We must use our will to make the choice and dare to sacrifice" the old for the new. With denials we do that elimination.

Exercise: Make a drawing of how you think denials and affirmations work in the "garden" of your subconscious program.

LESSON 4

Is there anything that can make my prayers less effective once I am in a Prayer Consciousness?

Consider Four Blocks to Effective Prayer

1. Unwillingness to forgive/a desire for vengeance.

Forgiveness of others and self is vital to introducing the full Divine Power into your situation. To forgive does not require forgetting. If we forget the experience, we might forget the lesson as well and find it being repeated. To forgive is to recognize that both you and the other did what seemed right at the time. Hold no desire for seeing the other harmed or punished, and no desire to condemn or punish yourself. If you understand that the offenders did what seemed right to them, then you might be able to find (not necessarily understand or agree with) the cause or belief in their mind that resulted in their thinking that their behavior was right. You cannot change another's beliefs; their belief system is their choice and their domain. The only alternative is to excuse or forgive their acting on their beliefs.

In the case of self or feeling guilty, which is to find fault with yourself, accept that you did what seemed right to you in the moment If you choose not to repeat that behavior, then you might be able to find the belief or the cause that prompted the action or thought for which you feel guilty. Even if you do not find that belief, it is necessary to accept that you did what seemed right at the moment, even if now you realize it was not the right thing to do. With the power of Divine Intelligence within you, you CAN change your own belief when you choose to do so. It begins with your will.

To forgive does not require putting or keeping oneself in a position to continue experiencing the same thing. It means to hold no sense of retaliation or placing blame.

2. **Fear of an outcome that is different from the desired outcome.**

This is a block to the most effective prayer because it sets up a resistance to the inflow of Divine energy.

Receptivity is vital in prayer. The first two steps of effective prayer are vital for helping to ease the fear and replace it with inner peace and faith.

3. **A false sense of personal power and determination in the situation is a deterrent to effective prayer.**

That attitude of determination takes back the personal will that you have surrendered to God with the prayer. It literally takes your "will power" back from God after submitting yourself and the other to Divine Order in your prayer request. This is evidence of a lack of faith or trust that Divine Order is for your highest good or theirs. The self-defeating attitude here is: "I don't want Divine Order; I want what I want." Divine Order is not a stopping point at which one must remain. Rather, it is a steppingstone from which you would make the next choice or decision. You could decide to stay there or to move in a different direction. A point of Divine Order is merely the most progressive point of order in one's journey of life.

4. **Impatience, a demonstration of weak Spiritual strength is a deterrent to effective prayer.**

Wanting to hurry the results without giving time for the dynamics to run their course toward the manifestation. This comes from not understanding that Divine Timing and the Dynamics of action are a part of the process of effective prayer. The action of cause and effect is not really a law but an appearance. The law is more complex than that. The energy that feeds the mind is of a different vibration than the energy that feeds the universe. In the mind, actions and their results in mind are governed by Divine Law, and in the field of energy outside individual minds, all actions and results are governed by universal law. Causes are merely actions, either mental or not. Effects are formations resulting from a combination of active causes. In any case, the law at work in the mind, determines how thoughts and feelings produce results in the energy field of the mind. The outer law, universal law, produces results in the outer energy field by magnetizing all energies within a specific range and combining them to produce effects. Your projected thoughts and feelings can contribute to the outer results as one part of the outer combined outer energies in a situation-thus an influence on the outcome-but your thoughts and feelings are not the only energy in that “mix.” Your contained thoughts and feelings are indeed the cause of your inner results, however. The ideas that you allow in through your outer attention automatically become stored in your subconscious. This makes them an influence on your thinking and feeling processes, but they do not control your thinking and feeling. What you believe controls your thinking and feeling. By acceptance or rejection, you remain in charge of what you believe and what you use as your expression of self.

A Quiz:

1. Q. What does forgiveness produce in the mind and what does lack of it produce in the mind?

   Answer: Holding a grudge produces a lower rate of vibration in the conscious and subconscious regions of mind. This keeps your attention attuned to the subconscious memory patterns and strongly conscious of the past. A higher vibration will block the negative or painful memory patterns.

2. Q. What does faith produce in the mind and what does lack of it produce in the mind?

Answer: Absence of believing produces doubt, not trusting God's wisdom, not trusting Divine Order, fear of the outcome. Having faith causes one to think about the desired outcome instead of about the problem.

3. Q. What does desire produce in the mind and what does lack of it produce in the mind. How does this relate to prayer?

Answer: Desire is the awareness of a valued potential. Conscious desire held in mind during prayer, produces open receptivity to the desired good. If what is desired is not in Divine Order or not in alignment with your progress on the journey toward enlightenment, it will not 17 be fulfilled. Absence of feeling desire in relation to that for which you pray is a sign of not trusting in its potential.)

LESSON 5

How can I know when the Guidance I am Sensing is from the Holy Spirit?

Choose God as the Guide and Senior Partner in your Journey of Life

1. Show your intent or will:

The mind can withdraw its attention from God, but the stream of God Substance that is within your individual mind is fed to you through the Holy Spirit, and it never shuts down. It radiates magnetic energy into every region of your consciousness at all times. The Holy Spirit is always ready and waiting to transmit your communications to God when you seek audience with God in the upper regions of your mind.

Once you have succeeded in experiencing the Divine Presence at will through the appropriate steps that lead to effective prayer or through certain types of meditation, you are ready to access and use the Wisdom, the Knowledge, the Guidance, and the Power of Divine Mind by mentally voicing your prayer to the Holy Spirit within.

2. Pray for guidance and accept the guidance.

A procedure for including God as the guiding "Senior Partner" in your life:

1) After basking in the Presence for a time, mentally project your desire for guidance into the Presence, (simply let your conscious mind communicate the desire for guidance into the Invisible Substance at the crown of your head, in which your conscious attention is immersed)
2) Wait in the Silence for creative ideas, impressions, or visions to come into your conscious mind. (Like a sponge soaking up the elements in a liquid) The visions, thoughts, and ideas that come while you are immersed in the Holy Spirit are God's immediate response to your prayer.
3) After your response from the Presence has slowed down or ceased, rest again in the Silence at the crown before closing your prayer time.

Trust the ideas that you received in the Presence, and follow-up with them. The guidance might be to wait, to act, to seek an outer resolution, to watch for opportunities or turning points, or to simply let it go. God is never harsh or demanding but gently informing you.

For one who is not accustomed to practicing awareness of the Presence before praying, it is more important to learn how to immerse your conscious mind in the Presence, than to learn the other steps of effective prayer.

That is why learning to practice certain types of meditation is so valuable. Practicing the Presence IS your experience of the Kingdom of God within you, the King governs His Kingdom and His Subjects by providing both Divine Wisdom and Divine Love Until we desire to experience the Presence and direct knowledge of God in our lives, more than we desire specific changes in the temporary conditions and relationships on our journey, we will be placing worldly considerations above our desire to Know God. Once we have experienced the Presence within and trusted in the permanence of that Presence, we begin to realize that this holy place in the upper-room of our minds is a place where God is the all-knowing One.

The superconscious aspect of mind within us is not God but holds the knowledge that God implanted in us. It is the area of mind in which we first experience the substance of the Holy Spirit and know the "Kingdom of God." We are privileged to visit that Kingdom at any time we wish, to pray or simply to enjoy the Presence.

We find that with every visit to the Kingdom of God we have a stronger and stronger subconscious memory and feeling related to that visit, so that not only the conscious aspect of mind, but the subconscious as well, begins to carry a constant experiential memory of the Presence.

Our attachment and love for that experience begins to grow in the subconscious, so that when the conscious mind withdraws its attention from the world and redirects it into the Holy Place, the subconscious celebrates that experience instead of struggling for attention.

Loving God and the experience of the Holy Spirit in the Kingdom, draws us into a habit of prayer, which is a giving in to the soul's natural instinct or hunger to pray and to know its Source. Gradually a sense of faith in God's Presence and availability expands in the consciousness. This is a result of repeated immersion of our attention in the Divine Substance; and we gain confidence that we can go there at any time. That knowledge stays with us day and night. Our entire consciousness is conditioned through repeated immersion in the Holy Spirit within; and it carries a perpetual conscious realization of God's ever-present gift of the Divine Intelligence within each of us.

We feel it in prayer more succinctly, but even when not in conscious prayer we have a subtle awareness of our own eternal life. We know that we, as living souls, are not our material bodies and that we are beloved citizens of the Eternal and Perfect Kingdom in which God is the giver and the receiver of any Love or Wisdom that we experience or express. God is the Substance, the Power, and the Creator of the universe. The universe is temporal; we are eternal.

If you want a specific outcome to your prayer more than you want to experience the Presence and the Wisdom of your Guide, you will hold that outcome as your priority, and you will find it difficult to accept any other outcome. You will find yourself arguing with God, saying, "What I wanted is good, and I asked for it in love, so why didn't it happen?"

When we let go of the belief that God will grant our every desire for good, then we will have our answer. God desires that you evolve as painlessly as possible but there are things for you to learn and understand so that you might become a co-creator of your own character and of your own life story in preparation for your home in higher dimensions. When you pray daily you can trust that you are in the flow of Divine Order for your life. Then you can use the power that God has given you for living your life in faith, and creative, constructive, harmless choices.

LESSON 6

Will My Prayers for Specific Outcomes Be Effective?

Choose a time and a quiet place to consciously meet with God daily and begin a habit of meeting God there just to experience the Presence and the Silence. Below is a highly effective type of prayer, but by no means is it the only way to pray.

Any kind of prayer is effective as long direct as communication with God is the intent of the prayer.

AN EXAMPLE OF PERFECT PRAYER

Divine Mind Prayer:
Six progressive steps:

1. Relax (close the eyes and relax mind and body)

2. Concentrate on the affirmation that God is always with you and in you. Continue to concentrate on that thought and let the attention drift upward to the Christ Center (Crown) Sense the peace.

3. Visualize or formulate in words your desired outcome. In this type of prayer, think not of what is happening or your situation, only of what you desire. Acknowledge that as the desired outcome or solution---not how it is to be accomplished. Form an idea or image of the desired outcome in your mind and let yourself sense how it would look and feel. The idea, image and desire will be your mentally spoken prayer or request to God in the Silence.

4. Invite guidance. Then wait in the Silence again to see if you get ideas about what you might be able to do to help produce your desired results.

5. Affirm the perfect outcome as a belief After this second time in the Silence, acknowledge that the perfect outcome is already formed in Divine Mind or in Spirit…example: “Divine Life and Love and Wisdom are now guiding me toward the right vacation spot to fulfill my need for a vacation. The opportunity is coming to me now.

6. Give Thanks This is a closing statement of gratitude. Keep it brief, like you would with a friend, such as “Thank you, God. Amen.” (Amen means “so it is”)

DIVINE ORDER EXPLAINED

Divine Order is perfect relativity on a progressive path of development for all concerned in a given field of energy. The universe is a field of energy.

Universal Order is a chaotic maze of disconnected points that sometimes lead to a dead end and always circle back to their beginning. The universe is one field of energy. It is a field of energy inside the wholeness of God. It is not God.

The human body is a part of the universal field of energy. It is in the universe and impacted by multiple factors.

The individual human consciousness or soul is a field of energy inside the human brain, but it is not directly a part of the universal field.

Its life-force of intelligence is fed directly to it through the connecting link of the Holy Spirit. The soul is not a part of the universe. It is "visiting," merely residing, in a physical body for a purpose related to the Divine Plan.

Divine Order is the ideal method by which the Divine Plan is being implemented, but an alternate way is made available through the more complex route of Universal Order**. Divine Order** is like an invisible "highway." It leads the soul directly to the fulfillment of its part in the Divine Plan through a number of development stages.

Divine Order is claimed automatically by the individual every time he or she prays simply by the action of intentionally including God as a senior partner on the way.

The result of prayer is always Divine Order, no matter who is doing the praying or how they pray. When we understand that our journey is like a lifelong dance with all of life and that a single point in Divine Order is like a steppingstone along our path, we know that Divine Order (or after-prayer circumstance) does not dictate our response or next decision but invites us to make it.

Our next order of business is to respond to that point of Order as a co-creator in "writing" our own life story.

God gave us a life so that we might live, as a unique expression of all the Truth, the Wisdom, and the Love that we can become. As we practice being all that we can be, and maintain our conscious communion with God, we are living expressions of our Truth, and the Harmony within us cannot be disturbed by outer, transient experiences.

The more we learn from our conversations with God, the more like the nature of God our thoughts, feelings, and expressions become as we are transformed.

When you stay "prayed up" your position in life is always on a step in Divine Order for you. For one who lives in daily prayer, that is the answer to the question, "Why did this happen to me?" That is because it is in Divine Order for you; an opportunity for you to become yet more conscious of God's Plan. Let your question not be, "Why did it happen?" but "What is my most constructive, creative response to this?" Divine Order provides an opportunity to respond.

The perfect response is to express your Spiritual character and understanding regardless of circumstances or situations.

If you cannot flow with Divine Order and accept it as a steppingstone for all concerned, your doubts will prevent having faith in God's response unless it is exactly what you prefer.

Knowing what you want is important, so that you know which direction to go when you respond, but to seek first the Kingdom is to want Divine Guidance and Divine Order more than you want to control the outcome. The demonstration of valuing that guidance is to accept that prayer puts all concerned into the right position for a next step, and to follow through with further guidance as you understand it.

If you can accept that Prayer always produces Divine Order in each situation, your feeling of appreciation will expand into a deeper sense of loving God, then to trusting God completely in perfect faith. Remember, you have but one life to live, your own.

When we try to "live" someone else's life rather than just share in it, we are misusing our God-given resources.

Examples of Praying for Specific Outcomes
such as healing, companionship, prosperity, safety, success, etc.

1. **Praying for Prosperity:**

Specific but not descriptive

Dear God, I pray knowing that all my supply begins in you. Doors of opportunity now open to me as I wait in the Silence for your guidance to the greater Prosperity that I desire. (Take time in the Silence to observe the processing of this request in Divine Mind)
Thank You God that my abundant supply is already manifest in Spirit. Amen

Specific and very descriptive Prayer for Prosperity:

Dear God, I pray knowing that you are aware of my circumstances and my need for $500 to have my car repaired. As I watch and wait in the Silence for your guidance, I see my good coming forth with the perfect and timely fulfillment of my prayer (time in the Silence to observe the processing of this request in Divine Mind) Thank you, God for your loving Presence and for abundant supply that meets my every need. Amen

Prayers for physical healing:

Specific but not descriptive.

Divine Life is flowing freely through every cell and every organ in my body. I am healed. Thank you, God."

**Important note: If this were said without using a name for God in the content it would be merely an affirmation, which is a*

White Magic activity that moves directly to producing results in the body and mind, but not necessarily in Divine Order. If it includes a name of God, and every name for God sets up a Divine vibration, it moves directly to the Holy Spirit, then to the Source, then into the body and mind to produce results. The "Thank you, God" at the end qualifies this statement as "prayer."

Specific and descriptive Prayer for physical healing:

Dear God, overflowing with your Divine Life, I absorb that Life into my intestines where perfect balance and harmony are restored to my digestive system. I am completely healed and purified of all evidence of disease. I now return to the Silence to receive Your Substance and I watch for your guidance, knowing that your Wisdom is perfect. Divine Order is now established in my body and in my life.

LESSON 7

How Does My Prayer Have Power in the Life of Those for Whom I Pray?

Exercise: With a partner or friend, Review the six steps in Divine Mind Prayer. Discuss the concepts below with your partner. If studying alone, write the six steps and write your comments about the concepts below.

A) After addressing God, the first force leading to manifestation of Prayer is the formation of the idea in Divine Mind and in your mind.
B) The 2nd Force leading to outer manifestation of Prayer is your follow-through with the guidance received as impression, images or ideas that come (you, acting as a co-creator with God in your life story)
C) The 3rd Force leading to manifestation of Prayer is the projection of your prayer from Divine Mind back into the appropriate point in the universal energy field.

D) The 4th Force leading to outer manifestation of Prayer is the action of the creative law as it merges the prayer actions related to the prayer request with the universal energies that are active in that situation, then projects a result to the targeted energy field.

Having attracted active vibrations, the 4th Force or creative law produces (gives birth to) the actual manifestation which is result of prayer.

The Manifestation of Divine Order

There is never a need to pray for Divine Order because Divine Order is the natural result of prayer. All else is universal order. After your prayer image has been transmitted back into the universal field by Divine Mind, your prayer has a greater potential to become a physical form or experiential manifestation than if you had not prayed. By experiential manifestation, we mean that:

- An actual form might be produced.
- A situation might form.
- An opportunity might arise.

- Or a change might occur, which has potential to lead to the desired experience.

Praying for others. The amplified Divine Intelligence delivered through the Holy Spirit is in every Soul, Using Positive Prayer to Pray with and for others, whether at a distance or up close, is just a matter of moving into that place of conscious connection to the Holy Spirit and acknowledging the eternal Presence of

God, then resting there until you feel a deep sense of peace.

Once you sense the inner peace of the Holy Spirit, you acknowledge that the Holy Spirit is also in the one for whom you will pray. A communication connection, like an invisible telephone line between your Holy Spirit and theirs, is established by letting your attention go to the Holy Spirit Aspect of the recipient as if joining with God in a desire for their good.

In a prayer for another, use the word "you or he or she or they instead of "I."

When including yourself in the Prayer, use the word "we."

Exercise: Read the following information with a partner or friend. Practice the steps with your partner, just to see how it feels. If studying alone read the information aloud and use your imagination to practice the steps.

Step 1. Relax in the silence. Example: focus your attention on the in and outflow of your breathing until you feel relaxed.

Step 2. Affirm the Presence of God and address God by name (a name of your choice): This opens the communication line between you and God, making you receptive. Acknowledge the Omnipresence of God everywhere at all times. Acknowledge the Presence of the Holy Spirit in yourself and the other.

Example 2:
Lift your attention as high as you can comfortably go toward the crown of your head. Think of God and say,
"*Dear God, we acknowledge your eternal Presence that is in the world, in the Universe and beyond. You are with us, around us, and in each of us as the Holy Spirit Within.*"

Continue holding your attention to the Presence by making a second affirmation such as: *We are now in the Peace and Beauty of your Divine Presence, and we rest for a moment in the Silence.*

Be quiet for a few seconds so that each person involved in the prayer can experience the heightened Faith and the inner peace that comes with it.

As you hold your attention away from the "tug" of emotions from the subconscious, the conscious attention begins to drift gently upward (perhaps envisioning light or pure energy, but that is not necessary. The Divine energy is there whether envisioned or not) At this point both recipient and prayer leader are more intensely aware of the Divine Presence Within than they were before the prayer began. This means that the mind is now divided between awareness of God and awareness of the "problem" or "prayer need," rather than totally focused on worldly matters or human relations.

Step 3. State and visualize the desired action or outcome. In this step the worldly situation is not mentioned at all, only the desired action and the Divine Powers that are capable of producing it. Concentrate on the intent or a mental view of the preferred outcome in progress. Let your imagination "daydream it" just as it is desired. Confirm the desired outcome with confidence that it is a definite potential. (You can be as specific or as general as you choose) State the "need" by describing the desired outcome, not by commenting on what you or the other desires to overcome… Why? With the focus of the praying person and the recipient on the intent, both peace and faith are increased in the recipient, producing a feeling of being supported and "not alone."

This peace and faith are different words for degrees of "wanting or receptivity." Wanting renders the body and soul receptive (open to receive), so that by the opening of the whole mind to receive, the conscious mind—immersed in Spirit---attracts the "Divine Life Force" like a laser beam to "cut through" or "channel through" the Holy Spirit into the receptive Conscious aspect of mind, stimulating the subconscious aspect of mind. The Subconscious Program, then responds with a vibration of harmony and receptivity that triggers the nervous systems and carries that Divine Power of Life into every organ and every cell in the body.

If we pray for a specific area of the body to be healed, then the channel will be focused more specifically on that area, but not limited to that area.

Example #1, step 3: (overall prayer for healing) *Now, in the Silence, we pray knowing that your Wonderful Presence and Power is restoring all things to perfect order in ( ) Life and affairs. The Life Force of God is everywhere, and that Life is now regenerating every cell and organ in ( ) body. Through your mighty strength (she/he) is healed Example #2, step 3: (prayer for healing of a specific area of the body) "(name) now receives your Eternal and Perfect Life force into her lungs. (he/she) breathes easily and deeply. With every breath (his/her) lungs are being regenerated and brought into the perfect function for which they were intended. She is free from all pain and discomfort.*

Step 4. Invite Guidance. Step 4 Example: *We wait in the Silence for your guidance as your healing work is being done.*

Step 5. Affirm the Outcome. This means to acknowledge that the result is already manifest in mind (therefore in Spirit) which is the first manifestation of all things. Why? Affirming the desired outcome is a powerful statement of faith and alliance between your conscious aspect of mind and the Divine Essence to restore and maintain the health of the body. (Together we will do it is the implied will) This is the unspoken commitment stage in which the conscious mind is agreeing to make choices and practice actions that support the claim to health, rather than defy or work against the life force in the body. The commitment to cooperate with his/her own desire.

Example **step 5**: *(name) is now filled to overflowing with your Divine Life. (he/she) is well and strong.*
Step 6. Give Thanks. Everything has already been said, and this is the point of closure. Make it short, triumphant, and confident.

Examples of step 6: *Thank You God, Amen* (Amen means "So it is") Example #2 *God, we give thanks now for answered prayer, knowing that your Wisdom is Supreme. Amen*

PRACTICE

Ask your partner or friend to state a healing need for himself or for a friend or relative. Using the six steps, create a prayer for healing and use it for your partner. If you are studying alone, pray for the healing of someone you know as if they were with you. Use the six steps.

LESSON 8

Other Effective Methods of Prayer

A true friend will not require you to avoid talking about your feelings when you wish to ask for help or advice. Neither does God dictate how we should communicate in prayer.

One highly effective method of prayer is one that asks for something rather than just describing the desired outcome. This is known as a *supplication prayer.*

An example of *"supplication"* prayer is the method that Jesus taught in the **Lord's Prayer**. Another example of supplication is the prayer known as the **"Serenity Prayer**."

Any request for that which is constructive and good can be used in this method of Prayer.

Lord's Prayer

The Lord's Prayer or "Our Father" is a series of affirmations that increase faith by inducing an experience of the Presence. These affirmations of acknowledgment, praise, and acceptance are followed by a request, ending with a closure. The steps applied are:

1. Relax
2. Acknowledge the Presence and offer reverent praise
3. Ask God to give you what you want
4. Close

Another method of effective prayer is just a statement of bold *affirmation*. It neither describes a desire, nor makes a request but boldly states that God's Presence is always in and around us and that the desired benefit is already available just by claiming that it exists. (I would add loud and clear that in order for this type of prayer to be effective we must be ever receptive to ideas and following through with actions that support the claim.)

An Example of affirmative prayer is the *Prayer of Protection* by Jim Freeman (notice it is not a prayer "for" protection but a prayer "of" protection. It indirectly acknowledges the danger in the world while recognizing the opposite potential. It affirms and assumes that the protection is already there.
1. The Light of God surrounds us. The Love of God enfolds us. (Acknowledging the Presence of God)
2. The Power of God protects us (in the absolute there is no need for protection which means that this is not an absolute statement but a relative one stating the opposite of feeling fear or vulnerability) *The Presence of God watches over us.* (a second affirmation to offset the fear of being vulnerable or alone in a dangerous place)
3. Wherever we are, God is, and all is well (a third statement that acknowledges the Divine Presence)

Note that this is not merely an affirmation of the Absolute, but of the Absolute *as it relates to worldly potentials for danger. The danger is not acknowledged, but it is suggested as a potential* by the word "protect," therefore it is a prayer of affirmation with both a statement of the Absolute and a statement of affirmation that the desired result is manifest. This method uses a very bold three step process:

1. Affirm the Presence by Stating that God is Present at all times
2. Verbally affirm the opposite of the negative feeling or the solution to a concern. State that the desired Potential is a reality.
3. Reaffirm the Presence the desired result.

EXERCISE

With a partner, name a negative experience or feeling, such as judging others, jealousy, envy, vengeance, sorrow, pain, depression, helplessness. With that partner, select one of the following Prayer Methods to use as a demonstration of Prayer for the opposite of the negative emotion that you named. If you are studying alone, use a combination of journaling and prayer for this exercise.

Supplication Prayer (This kind of prayer includes a request as if talking to God.)

Sample prayer for healing following Jesus' pattern: • Relax with attention near the crown of your head. "Oh, wonderful God, how beautiful it is to know that you are always with me. Restore the vitality of my body and uplift me with your power. (Take time to image this idea) Remove all that interferes with my perfect health and strengthen me to move freely and easily throughout all my days. (Image this idea) The power to heal is in you and comes from you. So it is. Amen

Affirmative Prayer This kind of prayer uses the vibration of a name for God, but it does not talk "to God." It merely states with confidence what God is doing and talks about God, not to God. It has only three parts.

How to create an Affirmative Prayer such as the "Prayer of Protection" Example using the emotion of jealousy Statement

Statement 1." The Magnetizing Love of God enfolds me, infills me, and expresses through me. It draws my Good to me."
Statement 2. "In my actions I am a radiantly beautiful, brilliant and a wonderful expression of the Holy Spirit. The Presence of God gives me confidence, assurance, and poise."
Statement 3. "Through the power of prayer, everything in my life is always in Divine Order."

How it works: The invisible image/form that is your prayer, projects back as a hologram into the universal flow with the addition of Divine vibrations. That hologram literally travels to a point in time/space where its further manifestation has the highest possible. Once it is there, it magnetically draws together all the active energies that are compatible with your prayer in that time/space. If there is enough mass of active energy in that energy field for the image to absorb sufficient power, the image will form a mass and produce a facsimile of the prayer intent.

Exercise: Consider the following and name some examples.

1. Prayer manifesting as form would be a literal physical result that everyone could witness.
2. Prayer manifesting as a situation would be the rearrangement of elements of the situation relative to your prayer, or the manifestation of a situation that seems "a miracle."
3. Prayer manifesting as an opportunity means that a strong potential will invite your participation.
4. Prayer manifesting as change in a current situation means that the existing energies in that time/energy field would take on a new relativity pattern.

When you pray, whether Mystic, Master, or criminal; that prayer produces Divine Order without fail.

LESSON 9

Difference Between Prayer and the Psychic Activity called White Magic

White Magic is not the same as Prayer, and I would not want to leave you without knowledge of the difference between the two. (Statements to contemplate or discuss)

Producing without consideration for Divine Timing and Divine Order. **White Magic** is a deliberate effort to mentally force into manifestation that which one believes to be good. It is done through Creative Visualization and the spoken word. (Or strongly repeated mental/emotional word if not verbal). The desired manifestation is not necessarily the best for all concerned, but the White Magician sincerely believes that it is.

When one is not willing to accept the potential that Divine Order would be different from the desire, or is impatient for the manifestation to develop, White Magic is the most positive alternative. It is a choice. There is no penalty for electing to practice White Magic in lieu of prayer, except that it might lead to paths and situations that are a deterrent to Spiritual progress rather than a straight path to evolution through Divine Order.

From the positive view, the practice of **White Magic** is the same type of harmless activity that we use when doing any kind of productive work without praying first. It is akin to any kind of positive or helpful activity that we do for others without the inclusion of prayer.

The final step in **White Magic** is done by turning the attention to the target of the effort or desire (whether self or another) and using words (mentally or verbally) to strongly state the intent while an image of that result forms in the mind. Once the image has formed in the practitioner's mind, he will use his focusing power like a laser beam to project that intent directly toward that target.

The manifestation occurs through a combination of the practitioner's will power, the degree of mental/desire energy empowering the image, the receptivity of the target, and the action of the universal law.

White Magic is not always effective. It can produce its results only to the degree that the target is in harmony with the intent. Prayer that is transported into Divine Mind through the avenue of the Holy Spirit within is always effective in that it always produces the highest potential that is available in the time/space that is related to that prayer intent. Prayer always produces a point of Divine Order, but the result of White Magic is limited to universal order.

Any 3rd Stage Race Conscious Individual (Neophyte/Mental Consciousness), or a Mystic at any stage, or a Spiritual Master can learn to deliberately manipulate the creative energy of his/her mind in conjunction with the universal Energy and universal Law to produce an exact manifestation of his intent. It takes a great deal of time and practice to be proficient at White Magic and few have the patience for it.

Black Magic is done exactly the same way that White Magic is done, only *with intent to do harm.* The creation power of the individual mind is awesome, and the Divine Intelligence within you does not dictate to you how you must use it. The Holy Spirit only inspires and influences toward good but does not control.

Learning to practice metaphysical manipulation is learning the Art of deliberate creative mind action, and it is a formidable and highly responsible practice. Black Magic can produce its results only if the mind of the target is in harmony with the intent. Fear and guilt are used by the Black Magic practitioner to invade the consciousness of an unsuspecting target.

Both White Magic and Divine Mind Prayer are creative activities of mind. White Magic can be dangerous in the hands of Psychics who are not Mystics or Masters. That is why it was a practice in ancient times that psychic arts were kept "secret" from the masses. In the hands of a 2nd Degree Mystic or a Spiritual Master they are harmless. Even if not doing intentional or actual harm, psychics who have learned the art of White Magic might use that creative power to gain fame, admiration, or adoration or to demonstrate for the purpose of material gain. A

Neophyte might use it for control or to make puppets of his followers for service to their own activities with a true belief that his intent is only for good.

Hitler is an example of a neophyte who was a practitioner of White Magic and later became so addicted to his power and fame that he turned to Black Magic.

His specialty was in the field of hypnotism. In the beginning of his leadership, he used his charisma along with hypnotic suggestion to influence the minds of his followers for what he believed was a good purpose. His original intent was to liberate European regions from what he conceived as oppression by their enemies.

Becoming enamored with his own charisma, mental power, and ability to hypnotize masses, he gave up caring about his impact on others and became a Black Magician intoxicated with personal power. He was a man so demented by his misguided reasoning, false understanding, and incessant focus on trying to understand the book of Revelation in the Bible that he perceived the Jews as the "antichrist," and the German society as

God's appointed liberators of the world from the antichrist.

(In the book, A Comparison of World Religions, see references to ancient Aryans who invaded India and became known as Spiritual leaders because of their ability to read Sanskrit and interpret the meaning of the Vedas to the illiterate. These Aryans were large people of fair coloring, and many believe that they were from the land that is now known as Germany rather than from Russia as is historically reported.)

Hitler's belief was that Germany was the elect Christian nation shown in Revelation and that their spiritual assignment was to rid the world of the antichrist before Jesus would return to earth. The burning that he chose in his madness to use for this "cleansing" symbolized God throwing the Jews into hell, with himself as God's agent in service to this goal. He believed that God would reward Germany by making it the ruler of the world. This might sound ridiculous to us, but it is not very different from a current day concept held by many that in the "end times" God will destroy all the representatives of the "antichrist" then the Planetary Masters and the supporters of the Christ ideal of “love” will be rewarded eternal life on planet earth, while the troublemakers are no more.

That is what a false belief with a focus on trying to control the world can do for a person or a nation. If the intent and purpose of the practitioner is to inflict harm on others, or to interfere with the path of others (even if thinking it is to teach them a lesson), this art of manipulation of universal energy is clearly the practice of Black Magic to various degrees.

Vengeance, driven by the conscious intent to teach someone a lesson or to hurt them through deliberately wishing or practicing pain inflicted upon them is a strong contribution to the destructive power in the universe. Whether emotional, mental, or physical, or to rob them of their right to make their own choices we can leave the outworking of that to Divine Order when we pray.

That is why forgiveness is the key to the most effective Prayer. One cannot forgive and still hold harmful, controlling intent at the same time; just as one cannot accept forgiveness in faith and still hold a sense of guilt at the same time. As we receive forgiveness from self or others or God, the guilty feeling is swept away and a sense of being acceptable takes its place. Many people find themselves being overly impressed with seeming "miracles" that someone is able to produce and believing that anyone who can intentionally produce such miracles must be a Spiritual Master. Be cautious. Both Divine Mind Prayer and White Magic are practiced intentionally by Spiritual Masters, but the responsibility of practicing White Magic is great, therefore it is never employed as a game or showing off a Master's creative power but always for an especially important purpose. The Spiritual Master is aware of the difference and for most the practice of White Magic is done strictly in private and rarely would permit witnesses to any "miracles" they might produce. If you see someone showing off the power to produce "something from nothing," just for entertainment or to "demonstrate their spirituality," that is not a Spiritual Master, but a talented *Practitioner of White Magic.*

LESSON 10

Actualizing the Holy Spirit

The Holy Spirit in you draws an idea into your consciousness that stimulates in you a passionate desire to feel and know that you are God's beloved.

There is nothing to fear as you proceed with your development and practice of the Truth as you understand it. The potential for everyone is that our subconscious belief system can be gradually transformed and fully integrated, in perfect harmony, with Divine Mind.

We can see Jesus as an example of the actualized Holy Spirit. (The ideals and creative powers of the Holy Spirit being expressed through his unique character and personality in the living of his mission) Through your willingness to be taught and guided by the Holy Spirit in you, you receive a conscious realization that God's creative and transforming Powers are contained in your mind for the purpose of applying them in your individual practice of living and thinking and being.

The Creative Divine Power is Divine Intelligence. Consciousness is but one of its Divine Powers, therefore the Source from which it comes is also conscious. The life force of that intelligence is in all things but only those things that have a mind as a part of their system can experience consciousness. The brain is not the mind but the housing of the mind. The brain is made active by the mind that occupies it, not the other way around. That is to say, the Divine Intelligence produces consciousness (Light) in the mind or soul; then the soul, when in a physical body, produces consciousness in the brain.

The Divine Intelligence produces consciousness of the individual self, consciousness of the Holy Spirit in your being, and consciousness of the Source from which you---with your inner Holy Spirit--- -have been projected into action. The Master, Jesus, prayed that his students would become more conscious of the

Source so they might feel energized and strengthened to do the activity that the Holy Spirit empowered them to do.

Do you pray for the courage, and strength and power to follow through with the ideas that come to you in prayer? Jesus prayed that the experience of the Holy Spirit would change his students from believing to knowing that the Power of God (which can be experienced and expressed as Divine Peace, Divine Knowledge, Divine Love, Divine Life, Divine Strength, or other Divine Powers) is in them and readily available to be used in their process of living.

When we pray, we are uniting our individual soul, through use of our Divine Intelligence, with the consciousness of God and the Divine Plan. In that process, our Divine Intelligence is amplified, and our prayer is absorbed by Divine Mind for a moment.

The prayer absorbs the creative power of Divine Mind, then is projected as a power-driven hologram back into the universe, right to the field of action related to our prayer (whether it be self or another).

In the universe that Power filled prayer blends with all other energies that are active in that field. Each of those active energies has its own “weight” or vibratory power as the energies blend.

The outcome is produced by universal law, and the result is always Divine Order for the target of the prayer. This means that the prayer energy in the blend lifts the active energy into a higher vibration that it would have been if not for the prayer.

Thus, the outcome is the perfect next step along the way in the order of that individual’s (or that nation’s, or that group’s) process of life.

Transformation toward the highest potential is the purpose for our existence, so Divine Order is a path that leads up toward the potential. It is important to realize that Divine Order is not a dictated or required path or position. To live is to move. On that step that is our Divine Order, we are merely in the best position to take the next step in our spiritual progress. The direction of that next step is our decision. We are free to choose to go in whatever path that step would take us, or we can choose to use it as a pivotal point and take a different path.

To stay in Divine Order for ourselves does not require holding to a situation that a particular step might place us on. It merely requires that we respond. The first response is your thought or feeling about the outcome.

If we are aware that this is Divine Order, we will respond in expression of the spiritual wisdom that we have gained to that point.

To stay in Divine Order, you only need to pray, then do your best to help yourself. A part of helping yourself is to accept the outcome as the perfect next step in the development of your life story and your Spiritual consciousness.

BOOKS BY MARY SAURER-SMITH

Windows of Life and Death
Spiritual autobiography of the author. A true story of consciousness development based on a Divine encounter at age three, two NDEs and numerous Divine Light revelations.

The Master Teacher Within
Presents 7 basic types of meditation from which all meditation techniques are derived. Each has its own limited potential, but in specific combinations they are limitless.

REALITY
Touches on all the concepts offered in the Keys to Enlightenment Program with emphasis on the Divine Plan and its Purpose These ideas will excite, surprise, and empower you.

Dynamics of Prayer
Prayer illumines the consciousness. Explanation of how prayer works and the effectiveness of various types of prayer. Examples and exercises.

A New You, A New Life

How to purify the subconscious of old habits and take a new approach to passionate living.

What Jesus Taught

In this book Jesus is seen as an assertive and charismatic master teacher, metaphysician, and mystic. Gospel reports are examined to expose the vast difference between the teachings of the apostles and the direct teachings of Jesus as recorded in the Gospels.

A Comparison of World Religions

First published in 2005 Promotes the understanding that all religions are belief systems presented by the founders of their religions. This book on world religions is unusual as it examines the life of the founder of each religion and how the religion developed. Available to order online through Amazon.com or Xlibris.com.

www.ingramcontent.com/pod-product-compliance
Lightning Source LLC
LaVergne TN
LVHW050602160826
845677LV00011B/2424

* 9 7 9 8 3 7 5 5 7 0 5 0 1 *